Palmistrı

MW01290368

LEARN HOW TO READ YOUR PALMS, AND START FORTUNE TELLING

By Mia Rose

Table Of Contents

Conclusion

Preview Of Spirit Guides - The Complete Guide To Contacting Your Spirit Guide And Communicating With The Spirit World!

Check Out My Other Books

About the Author

Introduction

I want to thank you and congratulate you for downloading the book, *"Palmistry for Beginners"*.

This book contains proven steps and strategies on how to practice the ancient art of Palmistry.

This book takes you through the secrets of palmistry, which has been practiced for thousands of years. The book provides a basic, but very comprehensive introduction, in any easy to read format, designed for the complete novice. Looking at the shapes of the hand, the fingers, the lines of the hand, the mounts and the smaller lines and symbols that appear on the hand, the book covers all of the main aspects of this often misunderstood art. The book also covers a little of the history of palmistry and looks at the way in which modern science has found evidence to support the truth behind the ancient art of telling fortunes through the palm!

Thanks again for downloading this book, I hope you enjoy it!

Chapter 1

Palmistry; A Short Look at a Long History

Palmistry – also known as Chiromancy – is a means of telling the future of an individual by looking at the lines, shapes and form of their palms. It has origins that date back, as far as we can tell, beyond recorded history. Although sources are unclear as to when and where the technique has its origins, it seems likely that there is an ancient connection with India. Some of the oldest texts relating to reading the future in palms date back over 5000 years to the sub-continent.

By the ancient Greek era, palmistry was already known in Europe and Aristotle mentions the technique in several texts. Aristotle noted that the lines of the hand "are not written...without reason" and he argued that they embodied both divine influence and, importantly, the individual's own nature. Alexander the Great and Hippocrates were both interested in the art or science of palmistry and contributed to the spread and popularity of the technique. Aristotle also noted that the "life line" on the hand could be an accurate way to establish the life expectancy of the individual. Although modern science has not made a great study of palmistry at least one modern study has drawn a strong link between the length of this line and life expectancy, stating that there was a "highly significant" correlation to be found between the "length of lifeline and age at death".[1]

By the middle Ages the art of Palmistry was an unquestioned source of information and many of the very earliest printed books dealt with the subject. By the eighteenth century, however, as the Age of Enlightenment progressed and promoted a scientific view of the world that discounted many

---

1   Department of Medicine, Bristol Royal Infirmary. Journal of the Royal Society of Medicine (Impact Factor: 2.02). 09/1990; 83(8):499-501.

traditional beliefs and practices, palmistry was beginning to be sidelined in mainstream society. Renewed interest developed in the nineteenth century not in small part thanks to the famous French fortune teller, Marie Anne Lenormand. Lenormand is believed to have read Napoleon's palm and predicted accurately his final defeat. Although a controversial figure in her time, Lenormand is regarded by many as having helped to revive interest in a number of traditional fortune telling methods and since her time interest and literature relating to palmistry and the art of fortune telling have continued to be extremely popular.

Although science – and many people – are largely skeptical when it comes to the "occult" arts of fortune telling, the basic rules of palmistry are fairly straightforward. Once you have learned these rules it's easier to judge for yourself whether palmistry is fact or fiction! The meanings that we'll explore in this book are devised from centuries of written accounts of palmistry and they, in turn, are the results of thousands of years of human study and practice.

The Basics of Palmistry

Even if you have never studied palmistry before the most obvious thing – and the one that you may have already noticed about the hand – is the wide range of shapes in the hands of different individuals. In palmistry these are separated into five different types, as follows;

- The Square or "practical" hand

- the Spatulate or "energetic" hand

- The Conic or "imaginative" hand

- the Psychic or "sensitive" hand

- the Mixed or "versatile" hand

In this first section we'll take a look at these hand types and the general character traits that they are said to embody. Even if you are unconvinced by palmistry, or have no wish to take your study of the subject further, you may find this section to be interesting and surprisingly accurate! The characteristics described can easily be used to compare against your friends and associates to see just how well they can relate to different individuals!

The Square Hand

This hand is easy to identify; both the palm and the finger tips are square in shape. Individuals with this type are both methodical and also very conventional in their outlook and acts in life. Appearances are important to the individual with the square hand; they will dress conventionally and will usually be neatly dressed and well presented. Individuals with a square hand value law and order; they are most comfortable when dealing with rules and regulations in life and will stick to these – sometimes rigidly.

The square hand is that of a practical person who perseveres in life to achieve solid, practical goals. Methodical in their approach, these individuals will follow instructions well. They are not usually creative in the innovative sense but can create in the sense of the craft-person or artisan.

Emotionally, the square hand may denote a difficulty in self-expression but a very strong sense of integrity, honesty and sincerity is to be found in this type of individual. It may take time for them to express how they feel but they will mean exactly what they say. Those with this type of hand will take things at face value and may, on occasion, find it difficult to see or understand perspectives that are not their own. Down to earth, practical and honest, they can also be intractable and stubborn at times.

The Spatulate Hand

This hand shape resembles a spatula or a small trowel, being broader at the wrist and tapering towards the base of the finger, which also appear to taper. In some individuals this pattern is reversed with the hands tapering inwards to the wrist, but in either case it is considered to fall into this particular hand type. The spatulate hand indicates an individual that is very practical but not without imagination. They have a great deal of energy and enthusiasm in life and are fascinated with ideas – especially new ones. Often scientists, engineers or inventors will be found to have this type of hand and anyone with an inquiring mind will usually have spatulate type hands.

Expressive and, above all inquisitive, the square-handed individual will make strong leaders, particularly in fields where practical work or projects are required. Along with science they can be found in the field of engineering and exploration. Irritability and dissatisfaction are the negative traits often found with this hand. The desire for new projects, experiences and people can make these individuals restless.

Emotionally they may be expressive but often hard to pin down. Not exactly afraid of commitment, they'll need plenty of new activities to keep them interested in one individual. They generally will have a wide and varied social circle.

The spatulate and square hand can often be found combined and this is a good combination. A square palm and spatulate fingers bestow inquiring energy and enthusiasm with a deeply practical ability to get things done in a simple way.

The Conic Hand

The palm in the Conic hand is medium in size and narrows noticeably towards the fingers, the tips of which are rounded but not tapered. This hand denotes a quick thinker and, to some extent, a dreamer. With strong imaginations, the individuals with this hand are often great talkers, happiest in conversation. They can grasp ideas very quickly and will be quick to discuss anything and everything. Their strong imaginations makes them very sympathetic to others, they can easily imagine what another person's situation or feelings are like. This makes them great friends in difficult times as well as in good times!

Loving music and poetry as well as art these individuals love to share their experiences in life. They are generous in every sense and love things of beauty in their life. Artists, singers, actors and public speakers often have this type of hand and they often possess a strong enough will to make a success in their careers. Where the Conic hand is combined with the square, the greatest achievements in artistic endeavors are likely to be possible – as the hand combines both the qualities of dreams and imagination with real practical skills to bring them to fruition.

Emotionally these individuals are generous, understanding and caring. They are expressive and understand their own emotions and motivations well. They are capable of being loving partners and make excellent parents.

Willing to be unconventional they also enjoy making life fun and will insist that you share in that fun!

The Psychic Hand

Slender, narrow and tapering to a point at the tips of the fingers this hand suggests a sensitive, idealistic and sometimes unrealistic nature. Those with this hand type are gentle and loving but deeply sensitive to emotions. They love beauty but often are neither practical nor possess qualities that fit them well for the world of work. Self-confidence can be an issue for this group, they do not understand rules or the normal order of the world, and this can lead them to depression or feelings of being outsiders or otherworldly.

When they find themselves in positive circumstances this type of person can be highly motivated but they often lack energy or the planning skills to achieve their dreams. At the opposite end of the scale they may quickly lapses into depression and morbid thinking, unable to pull themselves back out.

Although extremely loving, generous and possessing strong empathy skills, these individuals can isolate themselves from others as they feel the pain of others so acutely. The Psychic hand is considered traditionally to be the most "unfortunate" hand but it is also rare to see a purely Psychic hand. In many instances, this type of hand is mixed with other types and the square or spatulate hand can bring either practicality or energy to this hand shape.

The Mixed Hand

This type of hand is complex, despite the easy to understand name! Mixed simply means that it demonstrates combinations of the characteristics described above. Some examples have already been discussed in those hand types. However, the true mixed hand displays at least two, but usually more, traits. The palm may be of one of the four types already discussed and the fingers of another. More often the mixed hand will display a subtle mixture of several hand types, which can be identified by examining the shape of the palm, the fingers as a whole and the fingers in detail. Sometimes the shape will simply be hard to classify at all and may not fall clearly into any category.

The Mixed hand bestows versatility in many areas of life but no one single strength. Those with this type of hand may have many different jobs – even different careers – in life. They may flit from one interest or hobby to another and never really seem to settle fully to anything. This changeability may also be expressed in their relationships and they may have more than one partner in life – usually a series – although they may also be prone to infidelity.

Those with the mixed hand do possess great versatility and they may express this by considerable achievements in more than one area of life. Often they may achieve great things in their working lives and further success in another (completely different) field in their personal interests. Their abilities are often perceived as beyond the ordinary and with good reason!

Emotionally, these types can present difficulties. They have many interests and their relationships will only be one of these. Hard to pin down, either for life or for a date, they will often not marry or settle down in life at an early age.

However, they have strong abilities in many areas of life and can be incredible partners and parents who offer protection and encouragement to all those around them.

Reading the Hand Shapes

The shapes of the hand, in themselves, provide the basic information on character, traits and potential. Just a brief study of these hand shapes and the meanings that they denote will give you a sense of the potential of palmistry. In the rest of the book we'll look in more detail at the other aspects that are used to read both character and potential in palmistry. The best known aspect of palmistry is the lines and reading their meaning but, for those wishing to study the subject in more depth, it's important to understand that all elements of the hand should be read in conjunction. The shape itself can be thought of as the framework or the "context" in which the other influences illustrated in the hand will work.

The Hand of Fate?

Unlike some traditions or "occult" sciences most professional palm readers accept that fate, while it may play a part in our lives, is not an absolute or given. Lines on the hand can – and do – change over time. When performing a reading it can be important to emphasize this. The shape, mounts, fingers, lines and even texture of our hands express our future but also our future potential. This can change depending on our choices in life. Our hands reveal our past and our likely future and can be considered a snapshot of who we are now and who we may become. In the following chapters we'll take a closer look at all of these additional elements.

Chapter 2

The Fingers

The hand shapes described in the first chapter of this book give us a good indication of the type of personality an individual possesses. Alone they can be a useful reference point for making an initial assessment of individuals we meet on a daily basis. To understand in more detail the nature of an individual the next part of the hand to examine is the fingers. We'll look in detail at each in this chapter but before we do it's important to understand the meaning ascribed to each "phalange" of the digits. These represent the divisions of the digits by their joints. The upper phalange – that with the nail – relates to the will of the individual. The second represents reasoning abilities and the third, closest to the palm, relates to emotions and love.

The Thumb

The thumb is significant in palmistry in that it offers insight into background and inherited, or genetic tendencies, handed down from parents and previous generations. A firm thumb with limited movement in the joints suggests a narrower outlook on life and also a secretive nature. People with this thumb may appear very conventional outwardly but will often be less conventional in their thoughts or have a secret side that the world rarely guesses at. The firm, but stiff jointed, thumb also indicates a strong sense of outward appearance and concern with the way in which the individual is perceived by others. Those who have a suppler thumb with flexibility of the joints have a more open attitude to life, they may seem less conventional and rarely care too deeply about what others think of them. This does not mean that they are selfish – quite the opposite in fact - the supple thumb suggests an openness and generosity with others.

The Thumb; Length and Position

Longer and thicker thumbs indicate dominance and will power – but not without a clear sense of fairness and ability to use judgment carefully. The shorter and thicker the thumb suggest obstinacy. The position or angle of the thumb in relation to the palm indicates the level of independence and individuality in the individual; closer to the palm suggest a narrower mind, a conventional individual with less imagination than others. This often indicates a person who lives by the rules and prefers stability and tradition in many areas of life.

The widest angle of the thumb shows a character that is the most open, generous and with the strong empathy skills. These individuals are gentle, tender but may often be perceived as weak or easily taken advantage of. A very wide angle of the thumb suggests independence of mind and spirit; these people will take a look at the crowd – and then go in the opposite direction! Most people will have an angle between the two extremes and one which falls at right angles to the palm is considered to represent the best mix of independence, judgment and generosity in life, yet retains strong will power and the most balanced personality.

The Thumb; the Phalanges

Traditionally, only the first and second phalange off the thumb are used for palmistry. When both are of equal length this indicates a balanced personality who makes sound judgments and has a strong will. Both of these qualities will be in balance and neither dominant or detrimental to the individual or those that they deal with. When the first phalange is longer than the second this indicates a personality that is extremely determined but who has less sound qualities of judgment. They will strive to get what they want at all costs. If this phalange is also very thick it also suggests a strong temper, especially when crossed. A second phalange that is longer than the first indicates good judgment and the ability to reason and think clearly but less ability at carrying out plans and putting thoughts into action. These individuals are great when it comes to detail and organization but less good at practical application in their projects. When the second phalange is cut away in appearance, known as "wasted" in palmistry, this suggest a person of great empathy and tact.

The Fingers

The fingers indicate the mental and intellectual capabilities of an individual. Longer fingers demonstrate a love of detail. This will also indicate great analytical qualities and an inquiring mind. Where the length is excessive it may indicate a very strong ability at dealing with detail but limited abilities at seeing the "bigger picture". Short fingers indicate capable, organized and able administrators and teachers. These fingers indicate those who can see the big picture and are able to focus on this clearly to achieve their own aims and to aid others. Most fingers will be somewhere in between the two and the balance of focus of an individual's intellect and mental qualities can be determined by studying the length closely. Wasted fingers, as with the thumb, indicate empathy and generosity to others, in terms of intellect this suggest a desire to aid others through rational means. Short, wasted fingers indicate a teacher, instructor or motivational individual, who believes in education as a way to better the lot of the people they encounter in life.

The spacing of the fingers is important in reading the palm. Between the first and second finger a wide space indicates a broad outlook and independent mind. Between the second and third it suggests determination of spirit and the ability to overcome obstacles. Wide spacing between the third and fourth finger is suggestive of those who act very independently. On every hand the spacing between the fingers will vary; in the rare case of evenly spaced fingers the character is well balanced mentally and has the ability to achieve success in any area.

Finger Names

To distinguish the fingers in traditional palmistry the fingers are named after the planets Jupiter, Saturn, Apollo and Mercury. The first finger closet to the thumb is "Jupiter" and so on. These names are also applied to the mounts, which we'll cover later in the book. The finger of the hand that seems to dominate the others can be used to get a good overall indication of personality.

Jupiter

Where the finger of Jupiter is long enough to reach to the nail of the Saturn finger qualities of leadership are suggested. If it falls short of this point it's likely to indicate a dislike of leadership, management or responsibility. A crooked or bent finger of Jupiter demonstrates the desire to achieve ends at any cost (and often at the cost of others) while a straight indicates fairness in leadership. On occasion, the Jupiter and Saturn fingers will be equal in length. This is rare, but indicates a strongly self-centered nature – often tyrannical or dominating.

Saturn

Where the Saturn finger is very long it indicates a serious nature that may possibly inclined to depression. The shorter this finger is in relation to the others shows a serious, but balanced nature, which is serious but capable of viewing life with much good judgment. Very short, this finger suggests a lack of seriousness in life and the danger of irresponsible or risky behavior. Crooked, this finger suggests and individual who is likely to look on the dark side of life and may feel life is unfair to them. Straight, suggests a balanced outlook and ability to take responsibility for their own actions.

Apollo

The Apollo finger is related to the mind, particularly in relation to artistic and creative endeavors. Long, this finger suggests a desire for fame and success in these fields, while shorter Apollo fingers suggest less creative talent or desire for fame. Crooked this finger suggest a conceited personality, with a desire for fame or celebrity at all costs!

Mercury

The Mercury finger is related to business ability in life. Longer it indicates promise and success in this area and short suggests lack of ability. Most fingers will fall between the two extremes and when reading the palm you should consider the relative length of each finger which indicates the ability to achieve practical results in the area of work suggested by that finger.

The Fingers in Relation to the Palm

The fingers are set in a line from the palm and the angle of this line indicates the ease of the individuals' path in life. Where the fingers are set in a level line this suggests an easy path in life. Where fingers are set lower or higher than the others this suggests obstacles (a lower setting) in the area of life that the finger relates to. Those that are set higher suggests ease in the area governed by the finger.

Chapter 3

The Mounts, Lines and Symbols

The palm itself has two significant and obvious features, raised areas and lines. The former are known as the "mounts" in palmistry and they are important when reading the whole hand. These mounts, unlike the lines, do not change through our lives. They indicate our natural abilities in the main areas of our lives.

The Mounts

The mounts are named after the planets; those below the fingers are named after the relevant finger – Jupiter, Saturn and so on. The mount at the base of the thumb is named for the planet Venus, that opposite at the other side of the palm is the mount of Luna. There are two mounts named for Mars and these are on opposite sides of the hand – one being above the mount of Venus and below the mount of Jupiter the other falling between the mount of Mercury and that of Luna.

The Mounts are ascribed the following meanings;

- Jupiter relates to both pride and ambition

- Saturn for responsibility and justice

- Apollo relates to the intellect, particularly the arts and science

- Mercury stands for ability in business

- Venus is related to the emotions

- Luna relates to the imagination and inspiration

- Mars relates to courage; there are two mounts in this case as courage can relate to two types – physical bravery and emotional strength

In a few individuals these mounts will appear to be roughly the same size and prominence. This indicates a highly balanced and highly capable personality in whom all aspects of the personality work together. This is an excellent combination but is very rare! Generally, one or more mounts will seem more prominent on the palm and these can be used to judge the nature of the individual and their likely potential in life.

The Mount of Jupiter

The mount of Jupiter relates to pride and ambition; balanced and well developed this indicates enthusiasm, self-respect and the ability to persevere. Over-developed this can suggest arrogance and a dominating personality. An under-developed mount of Jupiter suggests a lack of self-confidence. Where Jupiter and Saturn seem to join, or are both prominent, this suggests that the individual will find success working in groups rather than alone – though often in a leadership role.

The Mount of Saturn

A balanced Mount of Saturn indicates hard work, common sense and prudence. This suggests a serious nature but one that is fair. This mount often "leans" to one of the mounts next to it. Towards Jupiter it indicates a serious but very ambitious personality with the ability to succeed. Towards Apollo it indicates that the serious nature of Saturn will be lighter and, also, that an appreciation of arts and culture is dominant in the individual.

The Mount of Apollo

The mount of Apollo indicates creative ability. This can relate to the arts but it also indicates a mind that is open, creative and innovative and therefore relates to creativity in the scientific and technological fields. This is the mount of the writer or the thinker, the creator or innovator. The size and shape of this mount will demonstrate abilities (or lack of them) in these areas. Leaning towards Saturn it will suggest an appreciation of creativity but not, necessarily, the practical abilities in these fields. Towards Mercury it indicates the chance of great success in these fields, as the combination of creativity with business abilities suggest a nature that can create and sell!

The Mount of Mercury

Mercury relates to all matters of a financial or business nature. It is also linked to sense of humor! Business ability, charm and the ability to be eloquent are all indicated by this mount and will be possessed in proportion to the size and shape of the mount. The ability to make money is indicated by the placing of the mount; towards Apollo this is lesser (though will still be more than possible). The further the mount is placed towards the edge of the hand suggests the greater the money making abilities.

The Mount of Venus

The Mount of Venus relates to our emotions, to love and the home. Moderately sized, and not too prominent, it indicates a good heart, ability to love openly and a balanced and happy home life. Overly developed it indicates passion and often a love of luxury. Cold, introverted personalities are indicated by a less pronounced, or lacking, mount of Venus.

The Mount of Luna

The Mount of Luna relates to the imagination and inspiration. This is most prominent in the hands of artists and writers. An indication that an artistic nature is prominent is where this mount is pronounced and the fingers are well spaced. A low, or undefined mount of Luna suggests a staid, conventional mind, though these individuals will do well in business if the fingers are well spaced. A very large mount of Luna can indicate a lack of truthfulness is present; at the very least this usually indicates that the imagination dominates and the individual finds it hard to stick entirely to the truth!

The Mount of Mars

Mars indicates courage and the two mounts represent physical and emotional courage. That which lies between Jupiter and Venus represents physical courage while that between Venus and Mercury relates to emotional courage. The amount, or lack of courage, in both areas is demonstrated by the size of each. If that below Jupiter is over-developed it suggests the danger of rash behavior but, underdeveloped, demonstrates a fearful nature. The mount below Mercury suggests either emotional and moral courage, or the lack of it. The two mounts may be similar in size or differ, this indicates the natural strength of the individual and the importance they give to each type of courage.

The Lines

A short glance at most palms will show that they are criss-crossed with a maze-like map of lines. In palmistry it is common to give significance to five lines in particular, although many smaller lines are also used. In this book we'll concentrate on the main lines and also some common shapes that appear on the hand in relation to them.

The Life Line

This is a line which many people wish to have read quickly. It circles the Mount of Luna, running from the Mount of Mars to below the thumb. The length does tend to indicate the potential lifespan of the individual, though should be read in conjunction with other lines and the hand in general. A clear, long line suggest a longer life and good health. Weaker lines, or those that appear wavy suggest poorer health – though h in many cases this indicates nothing more than a need to be careful with health and fitness. Breaks in the life line indicated serious illnesses and the quality of the line after this point indicates the level of recovery. Where a break occurs and a square can be seen between the two ends of the broken line the indication is of a very strong recovery.

A double life line occurs relatively frequently. This has several interpretations and may indicate one or all of them. Many believe this to indicate a very strong constitution which will overcome any illness; others suggest that it is indicative a life-long relationship which gives the individual a deep source of strength. In this case, relationship can be taken to mean more than a love-relationship and this double life line can often be found in twins. Other sources suggest that a double lifeline can indicate two paths/careers in life. In all cases, the omen is taken as a sign of strength, protection and great ability.

The Head Line and the Life Line will, on most palms, start as one though they separate quickly. If the two lines remain linked under the Mount of Jupiter this suggests a sensitive, emotional nature. When the two are separate from the start, self-confidence is strongly suggested. As the two lines diverge the space between them indicates the level of adventurousness, or risk averseness, in the character. The wider the space the more adventurous the individual is likely to be. Where there is less space between the two lines, more conventional individuals with a fear of risk are indicated.

If the Life Line starts from the Mount of Jupiter this suggests the qualities of leadership and dominance in the individual. This line tends to run straight down the hand, rather than curl round the Mount of Venus and this suggest that the individual will have strongly dominant qualities.

Smaller lines that rise from the life line indicate improvements in either health or in terms of success. The direction in which these run will indicate where this success is likely to be. For example, a line running towards the Mount of Saturn will suggest success won through hard work and effort. Lines descending towards the Mount of Luna suggest restlessness, travel and a desire for stimulation through pleasure.

While the length of the life line is often taken to indicate longevity, many traditional readers take a slightly different view. A line that runs out to the middle of the palm before returning towards Luna is better read to indicate long life and vitality. A line that runs closer to Luna, however long, may suggest a shorter life. Where the Life Line runs to the middle of the hand and then returns, curling under Luna and the thumb, almost to the far side of the hand, many palmists believe this suggest very old age is achievable.

The Head Line

As mentioned above, this line normally starts joined to the Life Line. It indicates independence and confidence if it separates quickly and moves a greater distance from the Life Line. Nervousness and dependency can be demonstrated where it remains attached to the Life Line and does not move far from this line. A straight Head Line indicates a level headed approach to life, where the individual is practical and enjoys the good things in life.

The Head Line often runs straight and then turns one way or the other. Downwards indicates a person able to apply good sense and imagination to any situation in life and this is an excellent quality bringing contentment in life. Where the line goes straight across the hand, and dominates it, this can indicate strong intellect but lack of empathy with others. Curving upwards the line suggests the ability to make money – often through invention or innovation.

A short Head Line is indicative of lack of intellect and, possibly, a self-centered nature. The lack of intellect itself may not be negative, if balanced by practical skills defined elsewhere in the hand, and it's important to read this line in conjunction with these. A double Head Line is sometimes seen and this promises success and indicates unusually strong mental powers combined with the ability to put thought into practice. The space that appears between the Heart Line (covered next) and the Head Line, indicates an individual's ability to view life in either an open or closed manner. The greater the space indicates a nature and mind that is open, willing to change and to listen to others. Where the space is less, a narrow mind is indicated, usually this person will only see one view (theirs) of the world and find it hard to adapt to new situations.

The Heart Line

This line runs below the Mounts of Saturn, Apollo and Mercury. Occasionally this line rises on the Mount of Jupiter and this indicates an individual who will have fewer emotional relationships but ones that will be exceptionally deep and passionate. In this case, it suggests a person who may only love once and that love will be for good.

When the line rises from the Mount of Saturn this suggest several affairs and emotional relationships in life but rising between Jupiter and Saturn it strongly indicates not only a happiness in love but a friendship and companionship in significant relationships. The ability to be friends as well as lovers is perhaps the most important ability in long term relationships.

Occasionally the Heart, Head and Life Lines all rise together. This suggests an individual of great passion but with a selfish nature. Many loves may occur in life but few will be lasting and a deeper connection is rarely made with partners. A Heart Line that rises lower on the hand, below the mounts suggests unhappiness in love and a need to learn more self-respect before love can be found in life.

In some hands the Heart Line is absent and this is taken to suggest that the person finds difficulty in sharing life with another person. This doesn't indicate selfishness, in most cases but difficulties in connecting which may have roots in the past. Breaks on the Heart Line suggest the ends of relationships or connections with close friends. A strong Heart Line which runs clearly across the hand usually indicates one with the ability to love others with passion and with integrity, one who gives and accepts love freely and with good judgment.

The Fate Line

Commonly mistaken to indicate "fate", or outside influences, this line actually relates to success in life in relation to all matters of a worldly nature. It indicates the path of the individual in terms of obstacles that they may meet on the way to success. The line does not appear in all hands and where it is lacking it can be taken to mean that the individual will normally have a smooth, if uneventful, passage through life.

A clear, straight line without breaks suggests an easy path in life and the attainment of goals with effort but relative ease. The line normally begins at the wrist running towards the Mount of Saturn. If it runs right up to this Mount and across it towards the finger, the suggestion is that the individual will strive hard in life towards goals that are out of reach. Success in achieving goals is better demonstrated where the line ends at, or before, the Mounts. Where the line veers in the direction of the Mount of Jupiter it suggests that success will be achieved in life but through hard work and constant effort.

A line joining the Fate Line from the Mount of Venus indicates a strong influence on the individual by another. This can be a parent, teacher, partner or associate and is generally taken as a sign of help and support being readily available for the individual to achieve their aims in life. This line is one that often gradually fades over time after the influence wanes.

As mentioned the line should normally begin at the wrist but if it rises on the Mount of Venus this suggest that the individual will benefit from either influential friends or through inheritance.

If the Fate Line rises from, or after, the Head or Heart Line this indicates success in later life and often suggests that struggles in the earlier part of life will be considerable.

Breaks in the Fate Line suggest changes of circumstance; this is neither good nor bad but suggests that changes will occur which will have an impact on the individual's life. These can include career changes, geographical moves and marriages.

A Fate Line ending at the Head Line indicates that the individuals' path in life – and success – will be governed by rational and logical thought and action. Ending at the Heart Line the path may be strongly influenced by matters of the heart, or that intuition will play a greater role in their success.

The Marriage Lines

"Marriage" is the traditional definition of this line, or lines, although traditional practitioners simply saw the line as representing the number, quality and length of personal relationships, whether marriage was involved or not. The lines can be found below the Finger of Mercury on, or to the side of, the Mount of Mercury and above the Heart line. The number of lines indicates the number of times an individual will "marry" - and we can take this in the broadest sense of the word. Marriage lines occur regardless of whether an individual marries in the legal sense, in whatever tradition or culture. If they are absent it is likely that the individual will never become involved with a significant personal relationship.

The position of the lines in relation to the Heart line indicates the age at which the relationship will begin. Close to the Heart Line indicates a relationship beginning in the teens or early twenties. Half way up the Mount suggest a relationship starting in the twenties or thirties. At three quarters of the way up the Mount the relationship will begin towards the later thirties or, more likely, after forty. Later relationships will appear higher and closer to the Finger of Mercury itself.

If a marriage line curves downwards the individual will outlive the partner that the line relates to. Where the line ends in a fork this suggests separation (or divorce). Lines that curve upwards suggest that the individual will not marry or have significant relationships until they are older. The depth and strength of the lines suggest the depth of connection between the couple and are sometimes taken to illustrate the length of the relationship; shallower, less defined lines, suggesting shorter relationships while longer deeper lines suggest relationships that last for many years or for life.

Chapter 4

Minor Lines and Symbols

In addition to these five major lines discussed in the previous chapter there are a number of additional lines and marks that appear on the hand. These may or may not be present on the hand but can be significant by their presence or absence. In this final chapter we'll take a look at these features.

The Girdle of Venus

This runs from either Jupiter and Saturn to Apollo and Mercury, forming a semi-circle above the Heart Line. The line indicates a highly emotional individual who has a nervous nature and is subject to unpredictable moods. Most readers believe that if the girdle is broken this is a good sign. If the girdle runs to the side of the hand, rather than to the fingers of Apollo and Mercury, the indication is of an easily influenced person; this person may possess charm and be very popular but lack constancy. If the girdle does not appear it suggests a calm and well-balanced individual.

The Line of Mars

Found rising with the Line of Life and following its course (it can create a double life line and has similar associations) this line indicates unstoppable determination and courage. This line suggest an inability to give up and the ability to persevere (with success) against all odds.

The Line of Health

This is a straight line which can run from the Mount of Mars under Mercury, from the Mount of Jupiter or from the Head Line. It runs down the hand and may be long or short. It indicates care of health should be taken, rather than good health. If the line is absent this is taken as a sign of excellent health in life.

The Line of Brilliancy

This indicates outstanding success in life – far beyond the norm. Rarely present, it takes the form of a line which ends on the Mount of Apollo. It can, however, start from the Mount of Luna or from the Heart, Head, Life or Fate Lines. In some cases it rises elsewhere. Wherever it rises it will end on the Mount of Apollo and the point from which it rises – plus other lines it crosses – should be taken into account when considering where the success will come from and what field it may be found in.

The Line of Intuition

Rising on the Mount of Mercury and curving in a semi-circle to the Mount of Luna this line is rarely seen. It indicates a connection to psychic or spiritual abilities, to the other, to a deep connection with universal forces. It bestows deep insight in life and can be both a powerful line but one that can isolate the individual from society in general.

The Ring of Saturn

Another rare line, it indicates disappointment by constant efforts to achieve the impossible in life. The line forms a semi-circle below the Mount of Saturn.

The Travel Lines

These lines can be found crossing the Mount of Luna. Major journeys are depicted by lines running upwards from the wrist and lesser ones cross the mount vertically. Any of these lines which joins the Fate line indicate that the journey will influence the individual in a major way and those that run parallel to the Fate Line indicate worldly success brought through the journey. A cross at the end of a travel line indicates a disappointment involved in the journey.

The Bracelets

These are three lines which circle the wrist, they indicate Health, Wealth and Happiness and the strength and clarity of each denotes the amount of each that can be expected in life.

Marks and Symbols

These can be found located across the hand and may or may not be present. In most cases some will appear while others will not. They should be read in relation to their location. The most significant are described below.

The Cross

- On Jupiter; this indicates a long, happy marriage or relationship.

- On Saturn; superstition and a suspicious nature.

- On Apollo; disappointment in work or business.

- Mercury; dishonesty and trickery in business – either by or towards the owner of the palm.

- On Mars, below Mercury, problems brought by enemies in either love or in business.

- On Mars, below Jupiter; danger through physical violence, though it can indicate a military career.

- On Luna; lies and falsehoods may bring misfortune.

The Star

- On Jupiter; strong relationships and influential friends.

- On Saturn; good fortune through the misfortune of others.

- On Apollo; wealth but without happiness. If, however, it appears at the end of a Line of Brilliancy both wealth and happiness are indicated.

- On Mercury; Wealth through hard work and individual effort.

- On Mars, below Mercury, success and victory through fighting moral fights or for social justice.

- On Mars, below Jupiter, victory and awards in public life and this may well indicate decorations won through military service.

The Triangle

This will appear as a very definite form, small lines that are broken and appear to form a triangle do not count.

- On Jupiter; trust and success in public office.

- On Saturn; A deep interest in the spiritual aspects of life, most commonly found on the palms of those closely connected to, or working in, a religious setting.

- On Apollo; a strong and practical artistic ability; most likely found in those working in the creative arts and particularly sculpture or fine art.

- On Mercury; connection to, and interest in, public matters; found frequently on the hands of politicians and also journalists.

- On Mars, under Mercury; abilities to think and act quickly, in any situation. Doctors, nurses and medics in any setting often will have this mark.

- On Mars, under Jupiter; as above but likely to be found in military individuals and denoting a likely rise to leadership roles.

- On Luna; the ability to apply imaginative solutions to problems. Detectives or investigators will often feature this sign.

- On Venus; this indicates self-control and balance of personality, beyond the norm. Often found on those who care for others in some capacity, at home or work.

The Square

This is a sign which indicates safety and protection in some way.

- On Jupiter; this will bring protection against over-ambition and attempts to achieve the impossible.

- On Saturn; this lightens the dark influence of Saturn and suggests a deeply thoughtful but practical spirit.

- On Apollo; this brings level-headedness, the individual can achieve great things through the ability to remain calm.

- On Mercury; this protects against rashness and or/impatient tendencies.

- On Mars, under Mercury; safety and protection will be available against enemies in any public or business arena.

- On Mars, under Jupiter; protection from physical violence in any area of life.

- On Luna; this will offer security against fraud or protect those with an over-active imagination.

- On Venus; protection from passion or emotion of any kind, including rage.

The Spearhead

Appearing as either an arrowhead shape or three-pronged fork (similar to depictions of the pronged spear of the god Neptune).

- On Jupiter; general good fortune and luck will follow the individual in life.

- On Saturn; great insight and powerful academic qualities are combined.

- On Apollo; scientific or artistic abilities which will bring fortune through luck and opportunity.

- On Mercury; the ability to form convincing arguments quickly, a good speaker or politician.

- On Mars, under Mercury; an advocate for others with powerful skills in language and desire to right injustice.

- On Mars, under Jupiter; a warrior with exceptional physical bravery.

- On Luna; ability to find happiness in most circumstances and to create a loving and protective atmosphere.

- On Venus; protection surrounding the home and family, an excellent symbol on any palm.

The Grille

This is a small group of lines that cross each other, as with the bars of a prison cell and this image is relevant. In that it usually indicates where an individual may feel "imprisoned" in life, or rather the character traits that may be holding them back in some way.

- On Jupiter; pride and arrogance can lead to failure or disappointment.

- On Saturn; depression, anxiety or mental illness may threaten to hold the individual back.

- On Apollo; self-expression may come hard and the individual may appear superficial.

- On Mercury; the danger here is that the individual may try to accomplish too many things at once and fail to complete any project.

- On Mars under Mercury; being trapped within quarrels and small arguments can be a danger with this sign.

- On Mars, under Jupiter; a violent temper which will cause, potentially, real imprisonment.

- On Luna; this indicates a love for travel but, in this case, that travel may distract the individual from all other things in life.

- On Venus; obsession with love, or with one person, a warning of either unrequited love or of the fear of becoming involved with another.

The Island and The Circle

These two symbols appear rarely and both indicate a warning of becoming "cut off" or isolated in some way. In both cases they can be incomplete and this tends to indicate that the problems will be resolved. These symbols can occur on the mounts, the lines and even on the fingers. Their location will be key to understanding the meaning they impart. When reading the palm, if you encounter these signs, use the descriptions in this book to understand and interpret the meaning. The signs may not be bad in themselves but indicate an isolation in some part of life and it's important to remember that isolation can be overcome; often, these lines appear and disappear at different times of life.

Conclusion

Thank you again for downloading this book!

I hope this book was able to help you to understand the basics of the fascinating and ancient subject of palmistry. This book offers an introduction and there is much more to read on the subject but I hope that it has provided you with a solid grounding in palmistry and the basic abilities you will need to read your own, and anybody else's palm!

The next step is to use this book to uncover the secrets of your own destiny and that of your friends and family!

Finally, if you enjoyed this book, please take the time to share your thoughts and post a review on Amazon. It'd be greatly appreciated!

Thank you and good luck!

Preview of Spirit Guides -The Complete Guide to Contacting Your Spirit Guide and Communicating With the Spirit World!

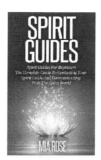

The spirit world is all around us, we are, in fact, part of it. Most people go through their lives with only a limited awareness, if any, of this wider existence. The occasional glimpse from the corner of your eye of somebody or something which isn't actually "there". Sudden, unexpected coincidences, which may be beneficial or otherwise. Sounds that may or may not be real, a door which opens unexpectedly and can't quite be explained away by the breeze. All of these are "signs" of the unseen, or half-seen, presence of the other planes of existence.

Here Is a Sneak Peak of what you'll learn...

•Shamans In The Eyes Of Our Ancestors

•First And Safe Steps To Meeting Your Guides

•What To Expect With Your Encounters

•Meeting Positive Spirits

•Dealing with Potential Negative Presences (And What To Do About It)

•Building Spiritual Relationships

•And Much Much More!

Check Out My Other Books

Below you'll find some of my other popular books that are popular on Amazon and Kindle as well. Simply click on the links below to check them out. Alternatively, you can visit my author page on Amazon to see other works done by me.

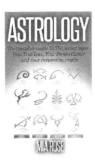

http://www.amazon.com/Astrology-Complete-Perfect-Personality-Horoscope-ebook/dp/B00N6HWV6K

http://www.amazon.com/Chakras-Beginners-Understanding-Sprituality-Meditation-ebook/dp/B00LNC6YGS

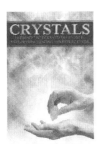

http://www.amazon.com/Crystals-Ultimate-Crystal-Healing-Spirituality-ebook/dp/B00SWMDP46

http://www.amazon.com/Numerology-Ultimate-Uncovering-Creating-Horoscope-ebook/dp/B00O6HWE8O

About the Author

I want to thank you for giving me the opportunity to spend some time with you!

For the last 10 years of my life I have studied, practiced and shared my love of spirituality and internal development. I kept diaries for years documenting the incredible changes that graced my life. This passion for writing has blossomed into a new chapter in my life where publishing books has become a full time career.

I feel extremely blessed and fortunate to have the opportunity to share my message with you! Each of my books are written to inspire others to explore the many aspects of their internal world. My goal is to touch the lives of others in a positive way and hopefully be the catalyst of positive change in this world :)

I am forever grateful for your support and I know you will get immense value through my books. I am really looking forward to serve you and give you great insight into my passions!

Your Friend

Mia Rose

Made in United States
Troutdale, OR
11/20/2023

14784658R00022